McLuhan's
CANARY

ESSENTIAL POETS SERIES 266

Canada

Guernica Editions Inc. acknowledges the support
of the Canada Council for the Arts and the Ontario Arts Council.
The Ontario Arts Council is an agency of the Government of Ontario.
We acknowledge the financial support of the Government of Canada.

Bruce Meyer

McLuhan's
CANARY

**GUERNICA
EDITIONS**

TORONTO • BUFFALO • LANCASTER (U.K.)
2019

Copyright © 2019, Bruce Meyer and Guernica Editions Inc.
All rights reserved. The use of any part of this publication,
reproduced, transmitted in any form or by any means, electronic,
mechanical, photocopying, recording or otherwise stored in a
retrieval system, without the prior consent of the publisher is an
infringement of the copyright law.

Michael Mirolla, general editor
Elana Wolff, editor
Cover and interior design: Rafael Chimicatti
Guernica Editions Inc.
1569 Heritage Way, Oakville, (ON), Canada L6M 2Z7
2250 Military Road, Tonawanda, N.Y. 14150-6000 U.S.A.
www.guernicaeditions.com

Distributors:
University of Toronto Press Distribution,
5201 Dufferin Street, Toronto (ON), Canada M3H 5T8
Gazelle Book Services, White Cross Mills
High Town, Lancaster LA1 4XS U.K.

First edition.
Printed in Canada.

Legal Deposit – Third Quarter
Library of Congress Catalog Card Number: 2018968520
Title: McLuhan's canary / Bruce Meyer.
Names: Meyer, Bruce, 1957- author.
Series: Essential poets ; 266.
Description: Series statement: Essential poets series ; 266 | Poems.
Identifiers: Canadiana 20190045809 | ISBN 9781771834063 (softcover)
Classification: LCC PS8576.E93 M35 2019 | DDC C811/.54—dc23

For Carolyn, Margaret, Katie, Kerry, Daisy

Contents

The Future, 1
Opening the Barrow, 2
Virginia Woolf, 3
Lu Mountain, 5
Losing a Father, 6
Candlelight for Moths, 8
Pipe Tobacco, 9
The Road to Alfacar, 10
Troubadour, 12
Freud's Waiting Room, 13
The Work We Do, 15
After Reading "The Window" by Raymond Carver, 16
The Iceman of Ötzi, 17
On Interring His Father's Ashes, 21
Alto Cumulus for a Teenage Daughter, 22
Coracle, 24
The Harmony, 25
Grenfel, 27
Abandoned, 28
The Pillow Book of Sushi Maki, 30
Bellwether, 31
In the Atrium of Royal Victoria Hospital, 32
Sewing, 34
Worry Stone, 35
The Picker, 36

Chives, 37

Clay, 38

Mowing, 39

Linoleum Floor, 40

Two Students on the College Lawn, 41

Dinner with Julia Kristeva, 42

Paper Plane, 43

Super Moon, 45

Janet Head, 46

High Summer, 48

The Art of Effective Umbrellas, 49

Oranges, 51

Red, 52

Pumpkins, 53

Air Stream Sugar Glide, 54

Garden by the Sea, 55

Egg Timer, 56

Arrival Time, 57

Wrist Watch, 58

Coyote, 60

The Jack Benny Radio Hour, 61

Definitions of Snow, 63

Snow Crabs, 65

The Commute, 66

Destinations, 68

My Father's Passing Contained No Poetry, 69

Moon Shell, 72

A Study in Grace, 73

Late Home, 74

Testament, 75
Meander Scars, 76
Palinode, 77
McLuhan's Canary, 78

Acknowledgements, 80
About the Author, 82

*Creatures of stillness crowded from the bright
unbound forest, out of their lairs and nests;
and it was not from any dullness, not
from fear, that they were so quiet in themselves,
but from simply listening.*

—Rainer Maria Rilke, "Sonnets to Orpheus"

*A dreamer is one who finds his way
by moonlight, and his punishment is
that he sees the dawn before the rest
of us.*

—Oscar Wilde

*You are waiting to hear its name spoken,
You have asked me a thousand times to speak it.*

*You who have hidden it, cast it off, killed it,
Loved it to death and sung your songs over it.*

—Gwendolyn MacEwen, "The Red Bird You Wait For"

The Future

My best coat sits heavy on my shoulders.
My best coat has many pockets,
and each is stuffed with what I carry,
with all I take with me to the future.

My coat is shelter.
I have taken you inside it many times,
pretended it is a house of tweed,
a dwelling place, a place of safety,

a shelter of pockets to warm your hands.
My best coat is way too heavy
as I ride a crowded, overheated bus
through the white-out of a December storm.

To either side of the narrow highway,
fields as white as the future spread
then vanish beyond a wire fence
that says there were boundaries once …

O, my love, what does the future hold?
My hands ache but there is only snow,
and whatever exists beyond the white,
beyond the familiar and the forgetful—

will it be a place that is part of us?
Will it sit heavily on my shoulders, too?
Will it have pockets to keep our secrets safe?
Will it be a shelter from future storms?

Opening the Barrow

in memoriam, John Montague

I find myself asking questions
about the voyage from life to death
and how light in a barrow corridor
awakens the beginning of summer.

I seek that light through winters
as it fights like a wave-struck hero
amid turmoils of the labyrinth heart,
and fumbles for words in all their frailty.

On the pavement of a sacred road
where waking only leaves more riddles
in the puzzles of the broken past,
we shall meet again at sunrise

when a ray of light strikes its mark,
and every word shatters into stars.

Virginia Woolf

On a summer day, I stood at the elm
and asked it questions like a traveller
inquiring the way to Delphi to hear
a breeze pass through the laurels.
I thought I heard an answer deep
within the dying bole, words flowing
as if a stream of bright colours:
a Bloomsbury map to the sea.

Silence is becoming in its own way—
country silences of rising larks,
the coded breaks of swallow songs—
a writer should never hide in silence.
Wind, sunlight, a summer afternoon—
everything in the Rodmell garden
desired to speak if someone would listen.
Speak to me life. Please say *yes*.

I know that behind the clever pottery,
beneath the layers of manuscripts
where not a single line bears correction,
beneath the stones that held her down,
and the ground that holds those stones
there is a privacy of thought one enters,
that place so like the silence within
it is a conversation between day and night.

There is one question no one dares to ask,
and that is the one about love,
the interrogative of reaching from despair
to ask for love's forgiveness in love's name.

I put my ear to the dying elm, its skin
aged, yet smooth and vital underneath,
learning to accept life's perfect imperfections—
how one moment flows into the next,

how the visions of what is possible
inhabit every minute, every hour of life;
how time comes to us all like waves
upon green shores and brittle coasts,
battering at all but what refuses to accede,
the stone shore, the passage of long seasons,
the heart beating at the centre of it all.

Lu Mountain

Closer to heaven, the hard slope brought us;
through clouds parting the way ahead,

a door of blue sky, the taste of sunlight,
our tongues lapping the thin mountain air.

In poems, a mountain is home to the sky.
When a spirit washes its face, rain falls.

When a spirit laughs at the overflowing basin,
the earth shakes to disobey the sky.

When skies darken, one must learn to love,
for every limit is the law of fathers.

My mother scolded me for climbing so far.
She followed me from her resting place

among the stones and fallen leaves, her face
still beautiful as clouds, tall mist opening,

the white air singing of a heart's long silence.
I shall never speak of mountains the same way.

My companions pulled me higher.
At the top, we searched for a sign of peace.

We laid stones we carried in our pockets.
Even the highest mountain needs to grow.

Losing a Father

Fathers always remind one
of what one is about to lose,
or lost, or should have lost.

Mine would stand waiting
and say it would rain before
I could get the mowing in,

and losing my place in a book,
I'd hurry and follow the beast,
up and down, back and forth,

the rawness of cut grass
clinging to me like a tail
before the daylight tired.

I lost my youth as he did,
lost a favorite heavy spanner,
lost a future where I might

have lost everything but
the self-respect I still have;
found and lost love,

and worse, a medal he won
and cherished. I even lost
the details of his face—

it has been that long and I
have lost sight of memories
of where we went or what

we did, the things we said,
his silences, and his moods.
I think I see him in my face,

in the way I see my own child
now that she has grown up;
and I see what I am losing,

her childhood and youth;
someday she'll lose me too.
I have a memory of his hands,

but have forgotten how to
change a jagged light bulb,
how to wire a new plug,

and his advice, if he gave it,
of how to make the current
run from him to me and on,

the life I thought I had but lost.
I still have my hair, but soon
it will cease to be important,

like losing something then
knowing it is lost for good,
if there is any good in losing

except for being a father.

Candlelight for Moths

Forgive the moths. The first
thing they learn as they emerge
from their cocoons is not how
to fly or mangle a sweater,

but how to dance. Their dust
from iridescent wings shines
like microscopic sequins
as they hover in the room,

divas in search of a party.
They make love to silence,
pretend to be the eyelids
of sleeping babies, the breath

of a flower as it closes with starlight:
the dance is their special talent.
Rhythmic in art and body they use it
to find the light in every room

to seduce a candle and its flame—
and when it touches wings
as a kiss seals a promise,
they know what they were born for.

Pipe Tobacco

The teeth of Napoleon's soldiers
recovered from a grave in Vilnius
bore the indent of clay pipe stems,
and rotting in a waistcoat pocket,
a bowl with shreds of a final smoke.
The blend was bitter as a frigid march,
the plume of an army fading out
in a wisp from Moscow to the Baltic,
their footsteps tampered like the snow.

Albert Einstein imagined them all
as particles of an expanding moment,
sketching their fragmentary glory
as a gift imparted by time and mass.
He fled Berlin and his humidor,
his tobacconist, his personal confessor,
whose blend, as sour as salty stardust,
was a bowl of burning bitterness,
exploding in the mushroom of a puff.

I prefer a plug of Mark Twain's mix,
an orchard of cherries on a riverbank,
blossoms as beautiful as boyhood's words,
where laughter in a plume of smoke
is the final applause of a comet's tail.
I see him ride it across the night,
whooping and hollering in a white suit,
as the smoke clears long enough to know
that everything must pass through flame.

The Road to Alfacar

They never found me?
No. They never found me.
—Federico García Lorca

Legend says Lorca is buried
in the folds of an old map,
a road that winds through
words the colour of red earth
after a gunshot no one
hears, the August air fed
with songbirds, crickets
crying *duende* in brittle grass,
where pages from a book,
turned slowly in the night,
are folded together as lovers
who refuse to part at dawn.
There are puzzles in the trees,
figs giving way to *brevas*,
fruit of forgotten moments,
tremolo of castanets, a pen
buried with the poet, a pen
timed to a dance of words.
A poet's words appear as daylight
eastward over grey hills,
a line scrawled on a blank page,
and on that line is written,
another world from nothing,
nothing mattering for nothing—
for little is gained by silence,

and to make more silence
is to make a grave, its earth
a forgotten home for strangers,
its rooms furnished with lost words.

Troubadour

A boy with a guitar
passed the house again,
the fifth time today.

It is raining hard.
Water falls in muted notes
from his six silver strings.

I cannot hear his song.
The window is shut,
and when I open it

he looks up, startled.
He begins to sing again,
but no sound leaves his lips.

He strums a chord
but his instrument is silent.
He smiles. He is dreaming music.

In a pathetic fallacy,
the downpour applauds.
Rain knows all his lyrics.

I will think of him
whenever it is raining
and hear music on the roof,

the sound of the world
believing its own beauty,
and every lie that makes it so.

Freud's Waiting Room

Upstairs through frosted opaque doors,
as clear as memories to keep things private,

you may be seated on the orange brocade
of armless arm chairs that try to hold you

the way your mother held you in her grasp
and told you all the lies of nature

you carry with you as a creed.
Believe them as you need to believe.

You will be forgiven, almost healed.
You will be succoured by the one you love,

the joke that helps you avoid your life,
the shadows beneath a banyan tree —

they come for you on an autumn night
when you try to mask your father's words

the way you mask the face of fear
when you think death isn't watching you.

Not the shadows, but the too-brief candles,
the lights you lit for your soul to read by,

and what they illumine will be your story,
the beautiful life you love for its lies,

a city of fictions, and streetcars, and cakes,
the rain that falls in fear of the sky;

for what keeps those secrets locked inside
are not the lies but the untasted truth,

the rhythm of footsteps on the long flight up
that remind you of heartbeats, perhaps a clock,

when time runs out and you have not been seen,
and you must carry your illusions with you—

a box of sweets and melted sachers
capped with cream like snow-topped mountains,

or the distant hills with chocolate slopes,
and the morning air that never sleeps,

or the night awash with coffee for dawn
that always belongs to someone else.

The world is a waiting room crammed with stories.
Its cure is the patience to tell them yourself.

The Work We Do

The day your poem was handed in,
some brilliance of the light outside
spilled on the page as I graded it.

Every word to me was daydream,
a country-scape of drumlined hills,
every flower spelled correctly—

it was so easy to picture you
walking among Queen Anne's lace
that blossomed in each sentence.

Today, years after your graduation,
after the world robbed you of dreams
to drive a person to sing of life

either in whispers or dandelion beards,
or claps of raving summer thunder,
I stare at the poem that astonished me,

the grade I gave as if rating an egg,
and pitch it out. Beauty is temporal.
Success is fleeting. Only memory lasts.

As it sinks amid the depths of paper,
I wonder if the bird in the final line
will light the meadow with its fragile song.

After Reading "The Window" by Raymond Carver

> *But at that moment*
> *I felt that I'd never in my life made any*
> *false promises ...*
> —Raymond Carver, "The Window"

My house is humbled under last night's storm.
I wait to see if the roof will buckle
because vicious weather carries a great weight
and art and storms kill what they celebrate;

and if the snow will melt, taking with it
the purity of the moment
I first saw sunlight on ice-coated wires,
when words aren't enough to speak of it
that asks me to see through a glass darkly,

I open my eyes in the middle of February,
half blind without my bifocals,
to convince myself that my frail and final failures
are but illusions of limitations
or a foretaste of some eternal mercy
that seem so impossible right now.

If I come out of winter with my mind intact
I will open the window and let the day inside
and declare that I will never again try to hide
the world and all its beauty,
no matter how much I feel its pain
when the ice finally goes away.

The Iceman of Ötzi

Having dreamed the sleeping thoughts
of three thousand years of winter nights,

his amber-coloured flesh reveals
the secret of what humanity became.

The cold-heartedness of each new day,
the icy temperament of those who live it,

shook him like a shadow from the future
as he fell into his stiffened body.

His eyes, long receded in their sockets,
were brown; in his age, the colour blue

only had meaning for a cloudless sky.
His weapons carried with him into death,

were meant to protect him from the chasm
from which there was no means of escape.

Everything about his walnut polished body
suggests he fought death fiercely the way

a hunter might fight for food, the beast
getting the better of his failing strength,

the ice surrounding him with numbing love,
taking away the sting of snow-capped dreams.

Even in the best of ages life is short and violent.
His body is marked with scars, recollections

of early medicine, gashes from feral teeth,
the claw-stains of overcoming nature.

Survival is a matter of collecting enough scars
to claim that life was a test of living,

and enough of a test to prove that failure
need only be victorious once. His thin arms,

made lean from having slept so long in ice,
his meagre legs and compressed rib cage,

belie the truth of wounds; that long before
anyone could speak of struggle as a temperament,

struggle made a man wary, broken, and old
before his time. For those he fought to feed,

the meat was never fat enough, the hides
never tough enough to last a long journey,

the spirit in the beast never wild enough
to make victory worth the effort of a kill.

He was an old man when he fell among the ice,
chased there by the footsteps of his life.

And if failure was not enough in his time,
he was discovered in an age when no one

dares to speak of how they fail, how words,
no matter how beautiful or strange,

as plentiful as fabled herds from stories
of the glacier's shadow side

are, in their half-starved state, insufficient
to describe sun sparkling like a million thoughts

off crystals spread to light his path.
His feet bled from the cold they touched,

his heels trailing red as if painted in a cave.
The higher he climbed, the easier it was

to follow him. Old men make it hard to hide
their thoughts from daylight. His path

only led his trackers to its pinnacle; at rest
he held his thoughts inside his sleep.

When they set upon him and he did not fight,
his journey took him to a wordless place.

Was he living when they cast him in the fissure?
Was he dreaming of words as fat as frightened deer?

And now comes the part that is hard to recite —
the dance of death's sleep, the frigid dark,

the silence that suffocates the legend in the man.
The longer he slept, the greater his awakening.

Look into the past where his eyes had sight,
into the palms of hands that touched time,

he holds his secrets the way ice holds winters:
he kept the cold as his companion through death,

his last meal analyzed, his bones and sinews
understood in ways he never knew himself;

he is a specimen of what has brought us here,
the truth of what we were and left behind.

He is a nomad in the wilderness of centuries,
measuring nothing but the life inside his dreams,

tracking the one creature that outstripped his will,
the secret riddle of what was and shall be sacred.

Look at him. He is not of the past but of the future;
he is the keeper of the afterlife each of us fears.

He is the man who, curled and foetal, waited
through our accumulated past, refusing history,

to be wakened when the shadow of fanged ice
opened its jaws. and there was hunger in us again.

On Interring His Father's Ashes

Algebra, whenever he taught it,
was about reducing large equations.

An outcome. A definite statement.
Each equal sign a new beginning,

another puzzle, that is not *what*
but *why*: why a river and a mountain

painted in watercolours as pale
as clouds resembles a new question.

In a Chinese landscape, the articulate
remains; the rest is cast aside.

What is not essential, the landmark
of a temple on a mountain side —

even the breath-taking valley view,
the thin blue wash of a horizon —

are neither the river nor the journey,
but what is lost — the silent monk,

his prayers, altar, and his thoughts
as clear and pure as lamp light.

Alto Cumulus for a Teenage Daughter

You sang until we drove into a white-out
on the long road home. Visibility shrank
to nothing, and the lane narrowed to lines
where the colours of a child's crayon book,
the kind we scribbled in to teach patience,
blended into the pencil grey of a fallen sky.

Fog is not merely a tired, settled sky;
it is a reminder that what climbed ran out
of sky in which to rise, lost its patience,
and fell to earth in a roadside grove. It shrank
from moonlight and lay as an open book
where you wrote *I can't*. The road's lines

are prayers for our safety, poetic lines
and glowing road signs; yet the fallen sky
is thin as the night air written in the book
life wants to write in a miasma, leaving out
the hard parts of growing up. I, too, shrank
from what I feared. It takes time and patience

to know there is something beyond patience,
a test by pain against strength, lane lines
to steer by in the dark. My big dreams shrank.
Growing up is like driving when the sky
crashes to the ground, and hides, shutting out
a future you can't imagine now. Time is a book

only you can write, and I pray that your book
will please you when you read it, that patience
will be your ally, not merely a virtue without
purpose. I, too, hated being a teenager: lines
and tethers held me down; life was a fallen sky.
Each day someone lassoed my cloud, and it shrank

beneath me. We all go through it, but if you shrink,
if you don't fight back, life will become a book
not worth reading—but I can't tell you that. Blue sky,
great thoughts, grand designs, and patience
are yours. Is the fog lifting now? Unwritten lines
on a blank page keep us going. This white-out

will pass. *You can.* Do not shrink from patience.
I could write a book of wise, useless lines, but you,
starry sky, are the author you can't live without.

Coracle

Should be the word for a chamber in the heart,
for it, too, knows the lapping of salt currents,
a lullaby's rhythm rocking the traveller,
the ocean's depths that are locked in legends.

My grandmother would sing me to sleep
with an ancient Irish assonance,
vowels rising from her deep heart's core,
as if they held the secret of her life.

Waves are cold to the touch of my hands
when I dip them in the tide at Innis Mor,
and the ache in every joint reminds me
a ring finger vein runs straight to the heart.

The Harmony

Nothing here goes silent for long:
not the birdsongs of an April twilight
or even the sound of a woman
humming as she peels potatoes,
and watches her children laughing
outside the kitchen window.
Their voices are footprints in the yard
woven into the first days of spring
when it rains and the ground is soft.
A dog barks in the night. A barn owl
questions itself outside her window,
or the wind in brittle winter starlight
finds its body trailing after it
as it listens in the eaves for heartbeats
growing fainter in the vacant house.
There are sounds the ear cannot hear—
noises that bend to the shape of absence,
an emptiness not silence but patience,
the long wait among fields and barns
for someone to return and love the earth,
as it was loved once by necessity,
to be there and fed with living voices
until it hungered no more;
for shadows to stand as they did
in the frame of lamp-lit windows
and the give and take of floorboards
or a hinge rusting itself to song—
nothing here goes silent forever.
There is a moment on a May evening
when it is possible to hear grass grow,
and catch the almost inaudible sighs

of the woman who stood at the window
as she wondered beneath her breath
what she would say when her time was over,
and she had nothing more to say.
Every blade of grass repeats her words.

Grenfel

The dog always knows
when we are on the road
to Grenfel. The concession
clings to drumlin curves
and slides into a hollow
before the last shred of light
has left the sky. Step away
from the car. The afterglow
is celebrating its silence.
The crickets hush. The sun's
remnants light your cheeks.
The dog, already in ecstasy,
her ball, glowing and yellow,
she races after it, fast as time,
and leaps with mouth agape
to pull it down like sunset.
And that is how time stops,
how it gives way to skies
of ribboned pink as old
as the stars it hides. When we
no longer count the hours,
there will be a small forever
holding the moment still,
waiting for someone to imagine it,
make it real, and fetch it
like the first bright star,
and lay it at the foot of night.

Abandoned

For those who observe emptiness
and feel sadness at a staircase

that has fallen from its reach,
or books wasting as words do,

a ceiling where branches let in rain,
or a bed where someone slept

and dreamed, perhaps afraid silence
would empty its mind into his

as sunrise at the foot of oblivion
shines when there is no voice in the mirror

to converse with the unknown,
and bars the way as if a stranger

arrived at the door in a storm
and begged to come in but was turned away:

for those who haunt the frequent past
because they cannot frequent the moment,

there is room for all. Your pleasure
is to furnish a space with heartbeats

of figures you have passed by night
in the doorways of city streets,

knowing the autumn in their eyes
will follow you to your place of rest.

Hurry home now. Rooms are waiting.
Switch on the light. Listen as it speaks.

The Pillow Book of Sushi Maki

We will dream tonight through tears
that taste as if we drowned at sea.

We will write upon each other's skins,
the thoughts of schools that never learned,

of *gari* and *wasabi* paste, *sashimi*,
and *katsu, teriyaki* and *gyoza*

shaped like pearl-choked clams,
and gems of fallen sesame stars.

Dream the words upon our tongues,
in blankets of rice and salmon skin,

the *wakame* hair of mermaid shores,
and waves in perfect cresting blue,

and mountains and their cherry trees—
for we are mouths that devour seas,

each attempting to turn the tide,
and what it changes, and how we change,

a leaf rippling a mirroring pond,
a dragonfly sailing on the curled leaf.

Do you see far shores in uncertain times?
Do you shudder on the crest of wind?

Bellwether

> *The leading sheep of a flock,*
> *on whose neck a bell is hung.*
> —Oxford English Dictionary

On that slant of new green hillside,
the sheared flock were grazing,
their nubbed wool as white as April,
they gnawed on tender tufted grass,
revealing stones beneath their tongues,
while ewes bleated a pastoral murmur,
and lambs sidled up to nurse.

In a pen beside the weathered barn
a bellwether spied us and was frantic.
He reared up as if a lion rampant.
A tin bell tolled around his neck,
its clapper clanged to warn the flock.
They paused but did not heed his cries.

We never talk about their fate—
about what should be on the tips of our tongues,
what is painful yet beyond all words:
can never imagine the slaughter that comes
the moment we turn our backs.
What blinds us to the truth of life?

Light was a blade between the fences
when we stopped to watch the lambs,
shy but curious in their easy trust,
their heads bowed as if they knew—
and everything I have loved in life
has disappeared beyond my words:
the feast leaves not a syllable behind.

In the Atrium of Royal Victoria Hospital

There are photographs of Dmitri Shostakovich
bent like a question mark over his keyboard

as he composed (a word for gathering up)
the dissonance of life in Leningrad besieged.

When bombs fell, and the city burned, he donned
his fireman's helmet, ash fluttering skyward

becoming notes in need of staves. Even birds
live on something, and cats in the Hermitage

were always hungry for flights of fancy.
He heard a clock chiming at four a.m.

despite the truth there is no time in wartime.
Today, the trees outside the Atrium

are naked as parallel lines, burnt and leafless,
the rear-guard regiment of vanished life,

soldiers surrendering to a paper sky,
voices starving, waiting for streets to fill,

peopled in the blink of a Russian spring.
There is no enemy save only time. Music

is the mirror of poetry, both random reflections
brought together, toned, ordered, disordered,

a state of health neither good nor bad,
a place knocked down to be rebuilt.

He believed in phoenixes and shovelled ashes,
paused to see black smears as notes,

played them with frantic ivory fingers.
The dissonance was his tribute to mankind.

After one long November night, soot on his face,
Shostakovich went home and asked how life

could survive arpeggios of anti-aircraft fire,
and stared out his window to the drum of bombers,

his reflection framed in one unbroken pane,
and determined to remake the art of order.

A man in a wheelchair with an i.v. bag,
sighs as he sips his morning coffee,

its steam twisting the tarnished light, its vapours
mocking our war with life, the battles won,

the advantages lost, the cup growing cooler
with each sip he takes. He smiles, sets it down,

says that it is good. He stares from the window
where startled starlings hammer a March sky,

and is in awe, a moment, at how his face is reflected
against the trees, their pale nodes of life.

He nods to me. Both of us almost died last night,
but today we live and compose our lives.

Sewing

Each darting plunge
like fortune's wheel —
the bobbin spinning
to her toe's touch,

her tongue locked
between front teeth —
such concentration
held our lives in check;

or when she'd baste
my sister's puff sleeve
or hung nautical drapes
to keep nightmares out,

she'd snip a length
as if to cut a cord,
then pull a seam
to test its strength

on a wear-worn dart.
Piece by patient piece,
she fashioned our lives,
a Singer, her delicate art,

racing to beat the light,
dancing on heads of pins,
repeating patterns by memory,
until the line held tight.

Worry Stone

My father's talisman for concern,
was rubbed green marble in his hand,

the hollow of its tourist gimmick
soothing in a patient, secret way.

Worry erodes the world slowly
the way life wears down mountains.

He could have worn a hillside bald.
If it was nerves, he was calm as stone,

but a hand in his pocket, a muscle in his jaw,
scrubbed like rain against the peaks,

for out of duty, or merely forethought,
came the storm clouds in his palm,

and when he died it was passed to me,
still warm as sunlight worries a dawn.

The Picker

It's no good if it can't reach
the high, round, red fruit
the sun burns in a summer sky.

It's no good if it can't catch
what it pulls with wire prongs,
careful not to tear the flesh

or hold what it cannot grasp
for wanting. It is the hand
of deliverance, the greedy clutch

that steals sweet fire from light.
It speaks to ambition and limitation.
It claims what lies behind the sun

even when the light is blinding.
The metal clasp handed down
one generation to the next, its grip

the warmth flowing hand to hand
the last time our fingers twined
and realized we came up short.

Chives

Easily mistaken for the shock
of stew divining on the stove,
still dew-covered beneath roses,
the onion breath was primitive.
Even as a child I wanted to wait
for it to ripen and be chopped
into the sunlight of egg salad
or strewn in green barber clippings
on mapled ham. By winter,
as the days grew tall and lean,
I imagined them as summer's nose,
pungent as the new skin I wore
when I walked behind a lawnmower
and chives echoed from my body.
I imagined summer as the season
I lost among the slender beads
of sweat abandoned in the night,
as if tears, clinging to green stalks.

Clay

When we'd had enough of shaping bowls,
we decided to see what human shapes

could do. If we'd written their names
on tobacco wrappers then rolled them in,

the clay might have stood up and walked.
In the heat, the river grey mud hardened

to dust and crumbled like a body;
and when we tried to take them home

all we had to show were soiled hands.
Playing God was little fun.

We were not great artists. We'd snatch
our inspiration in glints of rivulets

and leave the last man naked;
and when he walked abroad, crumbling

with each step and calling for his maker,
he asked why he'd been made at all.

Mowing

With a tea stain in the city sky,
the early hours of a summer day
were dusty and tired as the dusk.

I would begin my first real job
pushing my father's lawn mower
between trash bins on suburban streets.

Work is how one abandons childhood:
and coming home with a little change
was a demarcation close to manhood.

I needed the money for school dances,
a dollar to buy a girl with sweaty palms
a cool drink after an embarrassing song,

the space between us an arid desert
among the dry places of the known world
where rain waits centuries to fall.

Linoleum Floor

Learning to sing was breathing.
The mint of winter air
on a leafless, mapled street
barricaded by shovelled snow,

the sound of snow singing, too,
each snapping cold step a rhythm,
the drumstick hum of hydro wires
playing with energy:

everything tasted of music then—
dinner at my grandparents' house,
the scent of baconed meatloaf,
the nub of a brocade sofa,

forsythia-yellow kitchen walls
and the marble-green linoleum floor
were signs of life in deep midwinter,
like an African violet on the sill,

its leaves furry as a rabbit's ears.
I have lost my life so many times,
but cannot forget where I left it.

Two Students on the College Lawn

Leaving my office late after teaching
a night class on love poetry's spell,
I find two students woven on the grass,
their bodies pale as textbooks beneath stars.
They are studying each other's eyes,
exchanging words of wordless tongues
moving to speak without a sound.
It is a night when poetry is whispered,
the air as if a conspiracy of breath,
or a sigh of summer learning to survive
the outset of another term. I pass them
the way a shadow floats upon a wall
when everything is breathless, a night
when lovers learn what love is before
love cheats them of its mystery, a time
to feel the softness of another's skin
and the rhythm of breath against the world.
I envy them, lying there, silent and starry,
their futures locked inside their souls
as each eye reads the other's eyes
to see if ghosts of future knowledge
haunt them as they haunt each other.
Tomorrow, they will recall tonight
as the time they made poetry out of life
and spoke by heart 'til the heart stood still.

Dinner with Julia Kristeva

Dinner began with the evening's childhood
and ended blind with the world grown old.

It was the day after 9/11. Seven seals were cut.
The seventh and final wine was poured.

We waited for her to remind us of life,
but life had to be elsewhere and left early

to seek shelter from the uncertainty that made
absurdity burn to stubs like second candles.

A flame, small as a moth when she spoke,
flickered in a foreign tongue, its diplomacy

still solemn in the face of the fallen towers,
the dust slowly settling. Someone asked

what the future would hold. She shrugged.
I write this now because days touched me,

tugged me forward as if from a dream,
and know it for what it is when I rise early

and there is a mist clutching at fresh sunlight
in the park across the street. The light

is yellow and curious about the world,
and reminds me of my nursery walls.

Paper Plane

We used to fear the teacher's pointer,
its ash slamming to crack our desks,

the swoosh it made as it came down:
we were lucky to conceal our hands.

The rod had anti-ballistic properties,
could pick a paper plane from mid-air

as if a pitch thrown in the strike zone.
We tested our best aerodynamics

the moment the old man turned his back.
With the lift of steady dead-warm air,

it would level, glide, circle the fixture,
and hang there longer than rain,

its wings illumined to a paper ghost
haunting the chalky silence. When it

came down it had no owner. No one
would ever say who made it, who had

launched it, or how in awe we were
when algebra succumbed to physics.

When a perfect one landed on my desk,
I unfolded its jet-sharp edges

and wrote a poem on it about flight.
I got caught and spent an afternoon

watching my classmates' prototypes
rise from a school yard maple tree

and find their way to the stars. I wrote
my poem out a hundred times that day,

hoping the next draft would be better.
Time is a fog that grounds my flight.

The boy who made my paper jet
is nameless now, fallen into sky.

I imagine him soaring to touch the sun,
his wax wings delicate, lighter than air,

carrying him closer to his grand design.

Super Moon

for Leonard Cohen

Tonight, the mirrored light we read by
is not enough for us to know by.
Tonight, the starless dark demands
we learn to write by touch alone.
What we feel lies broken now
yet craves our hands to make it whole.
What denies the heart its voice
cannot deny our patient ears.
What we say is not for now.
What we say is for tomorrows.
Through gnarls of barren leafless arms
a sad, blue light in need of eyes
points beyond the winter depths.
The lake will freeze beneath us soon.
We shall walk on water there
as it holds us on the shining ice.
Let it be the light to see by
that guides us where we have not been.
Here are words we gift the moon
to sing the wonder of times to come,
to praise what gives our bodies shape
upon the fallen leaves we loved.
We traverse the barren noise of night.
We will voice one embracing verse
the tongues of darkness dare not speak.

Janet Head

I had a dream that summer was a web,
a linking of strands in a honeycomb
spun by a wolf spider on the screen
of our bedroom dormer. It moved
as if breathing-in the morning wind,
its grey-brown legs grasping threads,
and I wondered if it counted the days
of life it had until skies turned slate,
the sun sinking sooner and sooner
into the treed turbines atop the rise.
The day before we left the island,
we drove to Janet Head for fossils.
A north wind from Algoma found us,
the sky turned to wetted limestone,
and a child cedar stood in the shingle,
its boll and roots exposed to waves,
and I wondered if it would survive
to declare the presence of green life
when what we know is also stone.
My dream of summer had an ocean,
of corals fanning tropical seas,
living and dying for an ounce of sun,
and spreading as if they'd last forever.
They did. I hold their transcript
in my hand, a story of soft green seas,
a memory etched in stone to keep,
and touch, and wait to be touched,
to say the fight for life is never over,
each thought of life a recurring thought,
and you, pockets full on the strewn beach,
bending and finding a lost memory,

a honeycomb hardened into stone,
while a bee, focussed on the final flowers,
came and went and returned again
if only to leave something to the earth.

High Summer

The rain simply would not leave the sky.
It left the fields to burn between clouds.
It left the raspberries hard and bitter.

A few berries shrivelled on the branch
bore the beak marks of swallows and phoebes
frantic to feed their young.

Everything depends on something else.
I depend on you everyday,
and even though I rarely say so,

I return from the canes with barely a cup,
my fingers torn, red with blood and juice,
and I have few words for a dry season.

The Art of Effective Umbrellas

after René Magritte

Imagine going barefoot in the rain
or simply going barefoot in the rain

and the proposition of blending in
does not seem as normal as blending in.

One's umbrella should be at the ready.
Umbrellas are handy if one's at the ready.

Life a series of practiced preparations,
each daily ritual among preparations

is practice for a ritual life. Here is a street.
Among all the other long faces, the street

asks no questions. To be the least different—
a bright tie, a bowler hat, and what is different

is swallowed by clouds one carries in one's
eyes, the blue sky, the infinite pavement, one's

dreams and ambitions carried by time—
these things that matter little in time

are what make us formidable. The moment
when one does not pause to think of the moment

we have all eternity to do all that—
to be and do and be defiled by doing that

is what staggers us into what we are—
and what we are is what we are,

barefoot in the rain as if we just set foot
in the world while the other catches up, a foot

always one step behind, and in the rain
there are no footprints.

Oranges

I don't want to hear about oranges,
no matter how beautiful or sweet.

They are the widows of language.
Once upon a time, they had a mate:

their rhyme vanished. They kept
faith with a patient winter sun

settling in a bowl or peering between trees
so one could measure their shadows,

compare them to a harvest moon,
and think their loneliness strange —

the way a chord from a lost symphony
clings to the walls of a concert hall,

and footprints of old men on sidewalks
speak of history.

Oranges are the love I might have known
had I looked the other way in pouring rain

and felt the weight of a falling sky
press on my umbrella.

Red

Who would have expected my daughter
to choose the colour of angry planets,

the expanse of large, combustible stars,
or the port side light of a sailing ship?

She has seen it as she stared at fire
when the first autumn chill of summer

broke the secret code within a log.
Red holds emotional verities then blurts

them in a crowded room because passion
wears a bright crimson dress, and her lips

leave butterflies on a young man's face.
Red is the colour of becoming old enough

to know the difference between longing
and simple need, for it is the one hue

that possesses hands, either to hold a rose
or pluck it.

Pumpkins

They remind me of Emmanuel Levinas,
how he saw the face of God in every person,

how we seek it in small and mortal ways,
the image of something so like ourselves

it is impossible not to see the pain of moons
when they are round and cry with sorrow,

and we hide our children, disguised as ghosts,
so death will ignore the presence in their eyes.

Air Stream Sugar Glide

Around the curve, air hugged its skin.
Rivets would only cause a drag,
round heads thinking they can catch
a thread of slip-stream and hold on
because the world passes by too fast.
The air tastes of shoulder cinders.

This is how the country once slept
when it saw itself in polished armour,
when one gasp of reflected sunlight
was a benchmark on an asphalt map,
and those who read it searched forever,
knowing the treasure X was out there.

Hand on orbit-smooth of rocket skin,
time and travel still locked inside,
sweet as sugar on the long road here:
everything has to stop somewhere,
and here is but a line of thought,
waiting for sunset to say it's over.

Garden by the Sea

for Stanley Kunitz

Coming over the dunes I saw the garden,
the climbing pink roses, lilies,
beds of cosmos supernovas

and you, standing there, admiring
the handiwork you shared
with nature and cape winds,

the offshore floating through
strands of grey hair, your hand
raking them neatly into place;

and knowing who you were,
and I speechless and fifteen,
simply watched you as the sun

watches a season unfold in green,
or eyes scan the sea's horizon
for the right word to wash ashore.

Egg Timer

In these ways time is measured in departures:
the light on the western horizon at day's end,
the sift of raw red sand in the throat
when something inside hungers and needs
and cannot be satisfied with coddled words—
or the way a perfect song leaves the ear
and there is not enough of it to go round—
every note is a grain of red sand in a glass.
In these ways time is measured in departures.

> Are you watching the egg
> as it can be transformed?
> One instant it was tomorrow
> and now it is yesterday.
> A watched-pot never boils
> yet you live on miracles
> all you cannot see and faith
> that hides in its shell
> waiting to be tested by time.

As it arrives at the other end of the glass
those minutes-worth of particles the family
counted down through decades of memories,
the song everyone knows that holds enough
notes to be beautiful even when it is not sung
and the space between your breasts and hips
where I wrap my arms, and hold back time,
are the love and only love that holds back time,
as it arrives at the other end of the glass.

Arrival Time

A granite shoreline sealed his tongue
the way one snaps a watch-case closed

to keep a lifetime locked inside.
Winding the mainspring tighter than a prayer,

he set the hands to astonishment
to remind of the moment he arrived.

He broke his heart soon afterwards.
The timepiece ticked in another tongue.

The watch chimes every hour,
but no one can tell what it says.

Wrist Watch

When time finally grows older
it will learn not to break
other people's things — hearts,
keepsakes, bodies, and desires.

It will learn it cannot yellow
photos or old love letters,
tarnish silver, crush roses,
or steal the green from buds.

In a calm voice, it will speak
without rancour, will whisper
that some things remain
even when everything is gone,

and that beauty follows us
like a shadow in the dark;
that having held you I cannot
forget the memory of holding

what was so worth our hearts
it spoke to us not in lost days
but in the jewels we carried
strapped to our wrists, the winds

that moved over the beach
where we were the only ones
for miles on the level sands.
We took off our watches

not just to challenge the waves
but to break them with our bodies
young, and smooth,
and white as a waiting page.

Coyote

Bob's view from his kitchen window
should be a picture of silence
with only the glow and my shadow
spread on his wife's vegetable patch,
and the abandoned mosquito-proof
where we sat long after twilight
then made a dash for the house.
Locked inside, his field black
as ocean on a moonless night,
he asks if I want another beer
and pauses to squint at the corn.
He had spoken earlier of stalks
chewed and akilter —
I can almost see two star-points,
a vision as cosmic as fear itself
staring back at me from the crop,
its fangs blooded on a rabbit,
and run my tongue over my teeth
still tasting of the last cold one;
and I understand what sees us
from cruel safety, how it watches;
how it, too, considers death,
and what the afterlife might be
if anyone was certain it is there.

The Jack Benny Radio Hour

Last summer in New York City,
in a tenement gutted for a new hotel,
I woke chilled at three a.m.
having dreamed an entire episode

of the Jack Benny Radio Hour.
Rochester argued, a violin scratched,
the theme opening and closing
the show like the lid of a god's eye.

The view from the room's window
was a blank, black-sooted wall,
a Malevich square, no fire escape,
the way out entombed by time.

I have an old upright GE radio
my grandfather worshipped until he died—
when I plugged it in, Jack Benny
startled me through the static,

a rebroadcast on a winter night
of voices from the last World War
waiting to be heard again,
in the spirit of failed wisdom—

that death and time are illusions,
and what is heard is always here,
clinging to the walls like paint,
or papers sheaved in a *recollet*;

an archaeologist who put a needle
to the surface of a Mayan jar
and was certain she heard the song
of a potter working at his wheel.

It's not just that dead friends
still visit me in dreams,
or buildings long demolished
cast shadows they can't disown—

it is what the past owns
that refuses to leave this life,
the things that were loved once
that won't sign off their songs.

Your car is ready to leave now,
says Rochester. *Not so fast,*
Jack replies. *I need to finish
my cadenza.* (Laughter and dead air).

Definitions of Snow

The first snow each early November
is made of curiosity. It blows from the lake,

crystals rectangular, contemporary.
This is what is meant by *new*. The air

tastes of steel. After *new* snow when sky
blots out sun with a grief that will not

stop weeping for its lost children, clouds
come down upon sidewalks and cars.

This is called *whole* snow. It will not cease
until it kills us all. Or tries. Or fails.

Shout at *whole* snow and it will sound
the depths no heart has known, not since

last year or the year before. *Death* snow
comes in broad, heavy flakes

joined at their fingertips to wrap the world.
All hands but theirs numb at the touch.

There is no secret to *death* snow. Senses
are buried deep beneath it.

By mid-March, snow is pebbles,
a broken windshield, a view no one wanted.

This is called *pane* snow. It could melt
but it is far more patient. Its heart is ice;

but even ice and *pane* know their limits.
What is left by roadsides and in gutters

is *broken* snow, its brown hump a carcass,
a legend to describe to anyone who listens—

though they may not believe a word of it—
what it means to feel the hell from heaven.

Snow Crabs

The crabs *are* there, melting into
their familiar habitat, fallen on
zoology's harder times, patient
yet pure as the driven snow.
They are seldom seen by anyone
because no one ever speaks of them.
They are fauna's seedless Clementines
before the word for orange was said.
Like memory of what has no name
they bear the invisible weight of time.
They bear the silence of a hidden life,
the life they hide in like a shell.
Like a zodiac sign after daybreak,
or the silent truth below ocean storms,
they love in white and delicate bodies
masked from everything but a name
and multiply throughout the winter,
learning to sting in a veil of ice.
They count among the raw spring stars.
They pince the sun until it melts them.
A lone streetlamp cranes its neck
to count the diamonds of their eyes.

The Commute

A snow plough came by before dawn,
mounding the entrance to his drive
with road slush and the night's
inches weighted with ice and water.
He was behind schedule, his car
idling in the cold, chuffing exhaust
that took his breath away. He began
shovelling, lifting each scoop, tossing
the wall to either side of his curb cut,
adding to the rising rampart of snow.
By evening, the entrance would be
sealed shut. A neighbour heard
the shovel clang on the sidewalk,
saw him clutch his arm, then his chest,
his black gloves tightening, tweed
gathered in his fingers as he slumped
forward on the patch he'd cleared.
The herald of a police radio brought
the neighbours. They stood in pods,
pointing at the car, the driveway.
Someone reached in, took the keys
from the ignition. The air fell silent.
In the kitchen, his wife scrunched
a tissue in her fingers, blew her nose
a second time; the policeman shut his
report pad, and she shadowed him
to the hall. The ambulance pulled away.

She would follow later. She stood
in her door in a cloud of breath,
stared at the car, the shovel, and listened
as children down the block shouted,
one far louder than the others,
today was right for making angels.

Destinations

Think of ways to explain
where we are now on a highway

at midnight north of Toronto
as we run at a curtain of snow,

and standards on the median
are king palms ripe with light,

and lamps on the side-roads
are thin nuns bent at vespers,

and the stacks of dark factories
are men smoking in doorways,

and imaginary bridges float
above us to connect those places

that have not yet been imagined:
yet this is the way we find our way,

and everything is as real as love
and as determined to advance,

because what is true is true
no matter how it might be said.

My Father's Passing Contained No Poetry

1)

The rhythm of monitored hearts
and jagged lines struck like lightning
in cold, fluorescent, arterial halls
left me wondering if too long a life
had broken his heart in so many places.

On days when he sat up
to answer yes, or no, or not at all,
his food stank of its former selves,
yet he swallowed it the way one swallows fate
because he needed to say he had fought his end.

And the frosted windows were of no use.
They kept the world bottled up inside him
the way paradise is locked away in thoughts
or moments are torn from a long, hard night;

and I wanted to remind him
of days when we knew together,
a Cape wind scented with raindrop pine
mixed by the strong arm of salt air.

I wanted to sing old songs with him
and set him adrift among dreamers,
but the man in the next bed hit the floor,
and we both forgot the lyrics we knew
and how they melted like November snow
or a conversation we couldn't continue.

2)

Last summer in New York I rode a bus
from Tryon Park in north Manhattan
down Broadway in a greasy traffic jam,
the cogs grinding in the city's machine
waiting to burst into windows of starlight,
a million points in digital frames,
each one signalling that life goes on;

and the bus settled in the heat for an hour
among aging apartments in Washington Heights
until the street's slope prevailed
and we slid southward to the shores of Columbia
where he spent his summers among giants of
thought—

Hayakawa, Du Bois, and Buckminster Fuller,
the geodesic domes of futures to come
trying to shape tomorrows around General Semantics,
and I wondered what would have become of him
had life's practicalities not seized his soul.

I see him standing knee-deep in dreams
sparkling like fragments of shattered glass
a shop keeper sweeps on the streets of Harlem
because one broken window leads to the next.

3)

I'd give anything now to ask you questions,
but the last line you ever rode
straight as Broadway until it veered,
was a flat line disappearing in a maze
bound to be bent, made to be broken,
perhaps poetic, though a straight-shooter's quest:

and I try in my thoughts to add New York's ways,
the calculation of avenues and streets,
waiting for the sum I can never conclude;
and being the son who was bad at math,

I have nothing to offer except this gift:
it is poetry.
It serves no purpose.
It arrives uncomely as a hospital trolley.
It is footsteps down a cadeusial hall
where shadows robed in hospital gowns,
seek what they lost in losing life;

and taking my arm for your final walk
remark quietly, as if not breathing,
They could use some artwork on these walls.

Moon Shell

What survives, if anything,
is a pearled pink spiral
winding in on its own heart,
hiding neither the moon,
nor the shadow of my grandfather,
but the mystery that overcame them both.

Reaching low in the calmed shallows,
his hand would bend
in its refracted image,
and just beneath the sandy ripples,
would pluck a round, grey moon shell.

I have filled the chambers of my memory
with the story of fat summer moons
that swallowed the world to bursting,
then sank to the dark waves.

A Study in Grace

All the hidden things that give us comfort—
this bed that folds into a reading couch,

the breakfast you made and I ate quickly,
song birds that perch on your balcony rail,

a winter sun that watches from the south
and receives them—these are not merely shelters

but shadows we cast and leave behind
that no longer bear the weight of being loved.

Late Home

The key grinds its teeth in the lock.
The door opens. The vestibule different
than it was remembered. The shock
of familiarity revisited. The scent

of coats hanging limply on the hall tree—
being gone leaves too much behind,
and the details take their liberty
in the mind. All day travelling to find

that place where home belongs, the heart
at ease. Airports and train stations.
The power of the impersonal. The art
of not being oneself. The destinations

through which time passes until
a journey ends. With these and other
benchmarks, departure lounges fuel
anxieties. Waiting becomes the author

of fears. Home could answer that.
But the house is silent. Everyone asleep.
Even the dog doesn't notice. Hang a hat
on the usual peg. Set the shoes in a heap

of other shoes. Silently, up the stairs,
undress in darkness. The bed creaks.
The tongue has tomorrow and its cares,
and the happenstance of more mistakes.

Testament

The moon is shining tonight
for those who believe in moonlight,
and everywhere the light touches
is marked by a lunatic beauty
and I don't want to close my eyes.

Life is short. Poems make it longer.
I wait in hope that time
is just a bad joke being played
on a world eager for better things
and that better things will come.

I am not sad. Sadness cures nothing.
It refuses to recognize the joy
every shadow holds when the moon
casts light from the other side of tomorrow
and spills it as if wine.

Meander Scars

If water knew its own history
it wouldn't cut so deeply.
It would move forward
with the diligence of roads.
It would perceive time
as the pursuit of an end.
It wouldn't seek an outlet.
Conclusions rarely resolve
the damage done to reach them.
It would chart a course
of luck, seeking its fortune
in low places where elements
of air or earth or fire go,
and finding no horseshoes
to nail above the only exit,
would make its own apology
for behaving as badly as time.
It would sign its name as C
or double back in invocation
so only birds or clouds can see
it did not have a strategy
except to leave and then forgot
why it had to hide its story.

Palinode

They take it to work with them.
It follows them on vacations.

See it on their shoulders at airports.
They board planes with it and fly.

There is no shame in failure—
only self-doubt, the need to offer

an apology, an excuse, a reason
for having chosen badly and endured.

All this comes down to poetry.
Everything has to do with poetry.

This is what I chose. I live with it,
with words I cannot find fast enough

to describe the arms of a snowflake
before it melts beneath my breath.

McLuhan's Canary

Taj texts me as I lie down to sleep.
He says the sunrise over Mumbai
is goldly ancient with *muezzin* voices,
and his day begins as mine is ending

with moths buzzing on my window,
and the voice of a small world
crying in a dream I must bring to life.
Morning light on the Arabian Sea

is the colour of *azaan* filling the heart,
calling the world to its singular truth
as I pray that I will wake tomorrow.
The world lives one everlasting dawn

where time is only an illusion.
We no longer dwell in day or night
but in the eternity of a creative mind,
that instant when we think and speak.

It's a small world, my not so distant friend,
and we are brothers across beliefs.
A canary sings in a perfumed garden,
and Taj asks if I can hear it.

It sings a daybreak that will not cease,
in a world that cannot stop its turning.
I text him back that I hear the bird,
the song of a planet in search of itself.

Acknowledgements

"The Road to Alfacar," won the Gwendolyn MacEwen Prize for Best Poem in 2016 and appeared in *ELQ: Exile Literary Quarterly*.

"The Harmony," won the Gwendolyn MacEwen Prize for Best Poem in 2015 and appeared in *ELQ: Exile Literary Quarterly*.

"Abandoned," was short-listed for the Gwendolyn MacEwen Prize for Best Poem in 2015 and appeared in *ELQ: Exile Literary Quarterly*.

"Sewing" and "Snow Crabs" were short-listed for the Montreal International Poetry Prize in 2017 and appeared in *The Global Anthology, 2017* (Vehicule Press).

"McLuhan's Canary," was selected among the prize-winning poems for the *Lummox* Prize in 2017 and appeared in *Lummox*.

"In the Atrium of Royal Victoria Hospital," appeared in *Juniper — A Poetry Journal*.

"A Study in Grace," appeared in *The Trinity Review*.

The author would like to thank Porcupine's Quill Press, Black Moss Press, Exile Editions, Insomniac Press, *The New Quarterly*, *Arc*, Guernica Editions, and the Writers' Reserve Grant Program of the Ontario Arts Council for their support in the development and writing of this book. Special thanks to Michael Callaghan, Barry Callaghan, H. Masud Taj, Juan de Dios Toralbo Cabellero, Benjamin Ghan, Tim and Elke Inkster, Mike O'Connor, George Elliott Clarke, and Marty Gervais for their encouragement and support as this book evolved. My very special thanks to Michael Mirolla of Guernica Editions for this patience, belief, and trust in me as an author, and to my editor, Elana Wolff, for her brilliance and insight in shaping this book. My special thanks for the kindness, love, and devotion shown to me by my family: Dr. Carolyn Meyer, Margaret Meyer, my writing companion Daisy Meyer, my daughter Katie Meyer, and my wife, Kerry Johnston.

About the Author

BRUCE MEYER is author of more than sixty books of poetry, short fiction, non-fiction, literary journalism, and portraiture. He was winner of the Gwendolyn MacEwen Prize for Best Poem in 2015 and 2016, the IP Medal for Best Book of Poems in North America in 2014 for *The Seasons,* the Ruth Cable Memorial Prize, the E.J. Pratt Gold Medal and Prize for Poetry, and the Alta Lind Cook Award, and has been short-listed for the Raymond Souster Prize, the Cogswell Prize, the Gerald Lampert Award, the Indie Fab Award, the Lummox Prize, and the Freefall Prize for Poetry. His broadcasts on the Great Books became a bestselling CD spoken-word series for CBC Radio, and *The Golden Thread: A Reader's Journey Through the Great Books* was a national bestseller. He was the inaugural Poet Laureate of the City of Barrie and received the Barrie Arts Awards Lifetime Achievement Award and the John Graves Simcoe Sesquicentennial Medal in Recognition of his cultural service to the City of Barrie. Among his most recent works are the poetry collections *1967: Centennial Year, To Linares, The Seasons, Testing the Elements, The Madness of Planets,* and *A Book of Bread,* the anthologies *Cli-Fi: Canadian Tales of Climate Change* and *That Dammed Beaver: Canadian Humour, Laffs, and Gaffes,* the reconstructed lost World War One novel, *Cry Havoc* by W. Redvers Dent, and the short story collection *A Feast of Brief Hopes.* He teaches at Georgian College in Barrie, Ontario, and at Victoria College in the University of Toronto, and lives in Barrie with his wife, Kerry Johnston, their daughter Katie Meyer, and their pal, Daisy Meyer.

Printed in July 2019
by Gauvin Press,
Gatineau, Québec